OUTDOOR ROOMS II

QUARRY

OUTDOOR ROOMS II

ANNE DICKHOFF

GLOUCESTER MASSACHUSETTS

QUARRY BOOKS

FOREWORD BY JULIE D. TAYLOR

First published in the United States of America by
Quarry Books, a member of
Quayside Publishing Group
33 Commercial Street
Gloucester, Massachusetts 01930-5089
Telephone: (978) 282-9590
Fax: (978) 283-2742
www.rockpub.com

Library of Congress Cataloging-in-Publication Data
Dickhoff, Anne.
   Outdoor rooms II : more designs for patios, terraces, decks, and gazebos / Anne Dickhoff.
      p. cm.
   ISBN 1-59253-299-3 (pbk.)
   1. Outdoor living spaces. 2. Outdoor living spaces—Decoration. I. Title. II. Title: Outdoor rooms 2. III. Title: Outdoor rooms two.
   NA8300.D53 2006
   728'.93—dc22   2006012137
                                                                              CIP

ISBN-13: 978-1-59253-299-5
ISBN-10: 1-59253-299-3

10 9 8 7 6 5 4 3 2 1

Cover image: Conrad White/zapaimages/www.zapaimages.com
Back jacket images: Tom Bonner/Shubin + Donaldson Architects, top;
Bill Zeldis/Neumann Mendro Andrulaitis Architects, LLP, middle;
Tom Bass/ORR Design Office, Inc., bottom
Spine image: Courtesty of Warisan/www.warisan.com
Cover design: David Bullen Design/www.bullendesign.com
Book design: John Hall Design Group/www.johnhalldesign.com

Printed in Singapore

Contents

Foreword by Julie D. Taylor 8

Introduction 10

Opening Up 12

*Rooms inside the house that open up to the outdoors—walls of windows,
sunrooms and conservatories, and doorways into nature*

Finding Fresh Air 31

*Rooms that extend structurally from the house—porches, patios,
decks, and terraces*

Dining Out 60

Rooms for entertaining—outdoor kitchens and dining spaces

Expanding Boundaries 78

*Rooms that redefine boundaries by maintaining intimacy in open spaces—
courtyards, garden rooms, and pool surrounds*

Taking Shelter 108

*Freestanding rooms that provide a sheltered outdoor experience—tree houses,
gazebos, pavilions, trellises, pool houses, and prefabricated rooms*

Sensuous Essentials 136

*Outdoor necessities, from furniture and fountains to fabric and fireplaces, that
enhance the sensuous experience of your outdoor room*

Directory of Design Professionals 154

Product Sources 156

Photographer Credits 158

Acknowledgments 159

About the Author 160

Foreword

The outdoor room always seems to be the best of both worlds, spanning the divide between the great outdoors and the homey interior. Outdoor rooms are spaces where we can truly have it all: We're outdoors, yet sheltered. We can watch the world from a window, cozily snuggled inside, or be immersed within a grove of bamboo, as wild as the vegetation around us.

The best of these living spaces break down the barriers between indoor and outdoor, formal and casual. We let the outside whoosh into a screened porch, as it bursts with plant life, twig furniture, and atmospheric lighting. Or we let the interior take command of the patio with a full kitchen, bar, and dining room. Either way, we are in command of our surroundings, while enjoying how nature expresses herself.

The outdoor room is nature on our terms. You can balance an urge to connect with nature, with an impulse to control it by creating a room around it. When I perch on a bluff in Big Sur above the Pacific Ocean, I feel different from when I lounge on a terrace in Malibu. Both are exhilarating experiences; one wild, one tame. Neither experience is better, just different. No matter how well-mannered or refined, the outdoor room transports us, as the poet Byron said, by letting nature "sweetly woo" us.

Growing up in cities, my outdoor spaces consisted more of flat concrete than fields of clover. I broke out of my (literally) sheltered existence when I penned the first *Outdoor Rooms* some eight years ago. The most memorable thing to me was discovering how much people crave an outdoor connection, and will carve a natural haven almost anywhere.

Since then, as you'll see in this book, outdoor spaces have become even more full, complex, and inviting. Walls seem to disappear and interiors flow effortlessly to the outside. Adults are creating tree houses of their own. A greater integration of landscape and water elements further entwines nature and our living spaces. From the sparest to the most majestic spaces, outdoor rooms continue to resonate with homeowners and designers alike. I'm proud to pass the (Tiki) torch to Anne Dickhoff, who scanned the globe to bring you the next chapter in having it all.

Julie D. Taylor
Los Angeles

Design aficionado Julie D. Taylor is the principal of Taylor & Company, a Los Angeles-based public relations and communications firm specializing in architecture, design, building, and creative industries. She is the author of *Outdoor Rooms* and *Bars, Pubs, Cafes* by Rockport Publishers, Inc.

Introduction

The summer of my twentieth birthday, my grandmother bought me a lounge chair. It had a tan-colored, adjustable plastic frame and a pliable mesh seat. Beyond being a comfortable and very likable gift, this lounge chair was highly symbolic. It was my first piece of patio furniture, and with it I was assuming a place in my very own patch of the outdoors.

That fall, I moved into an old college town house with a covered patio and a grassy, sunken backyard hidden by a rustic stone wall and a row of crooked lemon trees. With my lounge chair, I spent many a sunny southern California afternoon on that patio having leisurely chats with my housemates, playing with our adopted stray cat, or doing homework.

Somehow, it was easier to concentrate on my reading with the sun on my shoulders and the wind rustling the pages of Jane Eyre, circulating the subtly sweet smell of lemon blossoms.

My lounge chair followed me from residence to residence, mostly for sentimental reasons. It sat on the tiny back patio of my first apartment and in my verdant poolside courtyard in Los Angeles, where pink geraniums spilled from brick-lined planters. Now the lounge chair is stationed in a corner of my comfortable Phoenix patio. This is where I go for a casual weekend breakfast, to experience the precious evening cool-down, and to watch jagged streaks of lightening crash on the horizon. In short, my lounge chair has inspired my several "outdoor rooms"—those places to which I can escape the static confines of the indoors and enjoy the pleasures that nature offers.

Though such spaces have been in use for literally thousands of years, the term "outdoor room" is a relatively new invention. It emerged in the early 1990s to reflect the growing importance people place on their outdoor spaces. The reasons for this migration outdoors are many—escaping the desk-bound lifestyle and connecting with nature, finding stimulating new places to relax with friends and family, creating a contemplative, soul-nurturing retreat—but the results are the same everywhere: people are treating their patios, porches, gazebos, and gardens with the same care they use in designing the indoor areas of their homes, bringing luxury furnishings and finishes such as kitchen appliances, water- and sun-proof fabrics, and elegant lighting beyond the back door.

This book will examine the evolving concept of outdoor rooms with photos of sensuous spaces from around the world. Though they vary widely in style, they share the same concept at heart. Whether Mediterranean-style or Asian, contemporary, or neoclassical, the rooms featured in this book embrace the sensory experience of being outside. Open arches and beams admit cool breezes and frame stunning vistas. Lush plantings fill the air with sweet aromas and natural materials, such as wood and stone, echo the organic allure of the outdoors.

Still, the term "outdoor room" is essentially an oxymoron. While being outdoors involves wildness and openness, a room implies shelter and intimacy. The spaces in this book gracefully combine the two experiences, creating in-between spaces that balance nature with artifice, wildness with control. Outdoor rooms allow you to feel the sun's warmth without getting burned.

First, we will tour the most sheltered of outdoor spaces—rooms that are indoors by strict definition but "open up" to the world outside through transparent walls that welcome natural light or walls that simply fold away to let in fresh air. Next, we venture just a few steps out the door to the spaces that extend from the house into the fresh air—porches, patios, decks, and terraces. Often contained within these spaces are elaborate rooms designed specifically for "dining out." These outdoor kitchens and dining rooms reach into the wild outdoors but are not so far from home to escape indoor luxuries.

While a room is usually defined as having at least one wall, outdoor spaces such as courtyards, garden rooms, and pool surrounds are "expanding the boundaries" of the traditionally defined room by creating intimacy in the open. Through flooring, flora, and furniture, they take advantage of fluid boundaries for protection and privacy far beyond the house. For "taking shelter" away from the house, people turn to freestanding structures, such as tree houses, pavilions, gazebos, trellises, pool houses, and prefabricated retreats. Whether fully enclosed or partially open, these spaces let you enjoy the shade without retreating indoors.

Finally, a look at the latest in "sensuous essentials" will help you to bring home the looks you love ... as well as the tastes, textures, sounds, and smells you adore. These products will help you create the best sensory experiences of all—your own.

Opening Up

Rooms are created to shelter us from the environment, but there is no need for them to shut nature out entirely. As people spend increasing amounts of time in sterile offices beneath artificial light, they desire a greater connection with the relaxing and inspiring qualities of the natural world. This insatiable hunger for openness and light is affecting architecture around the world. From modernist to traditional, homes are incorporating more glass and gardens.

The rooms in this chapter open up to nature and invite life through their doors and windows. From the shelter of their homes, owners can view the changing of the seasons, watch shadows creep across the floor as the sun sinks over the horizon, and listen to bird songs or the relaxing roar of the ocean.

◀ **BOORA Architects** principal Stan Boles designed his Oregon coast home to maximize outdoor views and natural light. Combining Scandinavian and Japanese influences, Boles uses organic materials, such as cedar-framed decks, pine-board floors, and fir wall panels, to blend the home into its natural, forested setting. On the top floor, spaces are arranged to admit light and ocean breezes. Floor-to-ceiling glass opens the living room to dramatic views.

▶ **Bright blue sky forms** a vivid backdrop for this urban penthouse where soaring glass walls bring the color and movement of the city inside. Deep red throw pillows and a geometric motif of yellow flowers on the coffee table contribute to the room's energetic atmosphere, while the order of the clean-lined architecture contrasts with the busy city, providing a sense of shelter and insulation.

Walls of Windows

"Nature is the art of God." Though philosopher Thomas Brown wrote these words more than 400 years ago, they still hold true for the projects in this chapter. Instead of traditional photographs, paintings, and wallpaper, these glass-walled rooms get their life and color from the world outside. Cottage windows frame sculpted tree branches. Colors come alive in the radiance of natural light, and rugged, natural wood and stone bring the outside in.

▼ **Sunlight bathes** this quiet sitting area. Architects Tichenor & Thorp designed the space with floor-to-ceiling windows through which shadows play on clean, white walls. A sensuously curving chaise lounge in rich wood counterbalances the stark lines of shadow and architecture, providing a comfortable spot from which to view the wooded area outside.

▲ **After witnessing the 9/11 attacks**
◄ in New York from a nearby building, the owners of this dramatic hillside home were determined to build a new environment where they could embrace life. Their new home welcomes in the surrounding city of Los Angeles, whose lights sparkle through soaring panes of glass that cover an entire side of the three-story house. Architect Steven Ehrlich designed their canyon–view contemporary living room. A plush rug softens the clean concrete floor, which flows smoothly beyond the wide sliding glass door to the patio outside.

◀ **This rustic living room** uses unfinished wood to blend in with its heavily forested surroundings. Curtains are hung along thick beams at half height to provide privacy without blocking light and views. Accessories such as the heavily grained coffee table, well-worn picnic basket, barrel-base lamp, and plaid pillows contribute to a casual country style.

▲ **Frank Lloyd Wright** is famous for building homes that blurred the distinction between interiors and the surrounding terrain. Shubin + Donaldson Architects embraced this philosophy when they designed a guesthouse to complement a 1938 residence designed by a student of Wright's. Nestled within existing oak trees, the guesthouse is a glass pavilion that opens up to mountain and ocean vistas.

◀ **Natural materials give** the interior an organic ambiance. A solid sandstone fireplace wall is anchored by a 35-foot-long (10.7 m) concrete hearth that extends beyond the glass borders of the house. A built-in Douglas fir bench lines the living room.

▲ **A mixture of formal décor** lends
an eclectic air to this sunroom. In
the dining area, a heavy British
Colonial–style table, laden with
elaborate candelabra, sits beneath
a florid chandelier. A wicker sofa
and easy chair, cushioned and
lined with colorful pillows, form a
more casual sitting area. A cheery
black-and-white tile floor reflects
the light that spills into the room
from every direction.

▶ **Natural light** and mountain
views provide inspiration for the
artist as he paints in his glass-
walled Santa Barbara studio.
Shubin + Donaldson Architects
set the second floor studio in a
grove of trees and use natural
finishes, such as the rhythmic
wood beam trusses and clear-
sealed plywood floors, where
strong grains and knots add
visual texture.

▲ **Exploring the nature** of boundaries was the impetus for this Nashville, Tennessee, residence. Located on a subdivided golf course, it sits on the boundary line between the city and the wilderness. Eric Rosen Architects capture qualities of both realms in the breakfast room—a glass-walled portion of the house that breaks the boundaries of its main massing. White-walled contemporary design exudes urban panache, while a picture window frames a water feature that extends into the wilderness.

Sunrooms and Conservatories

Framed almost entirely in glass, sunrooms and conservatories provide some of the best blending between indoors and out. Entire gardens composed of potted and hanging plants, or even plants sprouting from the ground, flourish in the sunlight. Resilient flooring materials—brick or wood for a warm feel, tile or concrete for a sleek, modern look— allow the introduction of water in fountains and pools. Garden furniture is a charming complement to the verdant setting, but some people prefer the contrast of upholstered furniture and luxury finishes. After all, there's no need for weatherproofing indoors.

◄ **Glass walls** and a vaulted glass ceiling give protection to the formerly empty space between this house and its outbuilding. The new sunroom captures flowering vines that climb the eaves of the two buildings, flowing seamlessly between inside and out. Lofty willow trees and thick hedges provide the room with shade and privacy. Inside, furnishings are casual, yet elegant. A scrolling willow branch chair and rustic wooden side table complement wicker garden furniture, while a metal chair and side table add sheen to the soft, natural palate.

◀ **When planning their sunroom** addition, the owners decided to incorporate a fireplace to make their outdoor room accessible year-round in chilly Illinois. Town and Country Conservatories designed a welcoming stone fireplace that ties in with the home's exterior and becomes a natural focal point for the space inside. Cushioned wicker chairs are positioned around the hearth to soak up the heat as well as the sunlight that pours through the vaulted glass ceiling.

▶ **Designer Stephen Woodhams** uses colorful plants and furnishings to merge this sunroom with an outdoor deck. A shaggy bright green rug imitates grass on the tile floor. The sculptural corner arrangement of birds of paradise complements the painted garden furniture beyond the glass wall.

▲ **Well-placed plantings** add drama
to this casual conservatory
designed by Town and Country
Conservatories. Sculpted trees in
terra-cotta pots form a grand procession down the long wall of the
rectangular room. The striking arch
of a flowering vine frames the back
window, where an overstuffed easy
chair occupies the place of honor,
accompanied by reading lamps
and a wicker occasional table.

► **Old and new mingle** in this
London conservatory, where the
addition of a glass box offers a
stark contrast to the aging brick
walls of the original home. Inside
the meditative room a sleek Le
Corbusier chaise lounge over–
looks a tranquil koi pond that
straddles the boundaries
between inside and out.

Whitewashed walls, antique wood, old-fashioned ceramic flowerpots, and natural stone flooring add vintage refinement to this romantic sunroom. The soft colors glow in the gentle afternoon light that filters in through the tall trees. Blankets are draped casually over the arms of wicker chairs and mismatched, ruffled pillows are scattered across their seats to create a sense of comfort. The crowning jewel of the room—an outdoor-style wooden bench swing—hangs in an intimate glazed alcove.

◄ **Operable stained glass windows** admit fresh air and filtered light into this French conservatory. Their rich hues of red, yellow, and green bring warmth to the room, and the curves of the wrought iron dining chairs add romantic appeal. Contrasting textures abound in this small space, from the upholstered settee against the wall to the organic, tapered sculpture gracing the center of the glass dining table. This layering of smooth and rough creates a rich atmosphere.

Doorways into Nature

Walls are optional in these least sheltered of indoor spaces, where architectural innovation breaks down the physical barriers between inside and outside. In warm tropical regions, open shutters and sliding walls bring in refreshing breezes. Fireplaces and wood stoves allow homeowners to enjoy the same outdoor luxuries in less inviting climates.

▲ **This seaside residence** blends the art of man with the artistry of nature. Its wide-open living floor houses high-end modern prints, sculpture, and furniture. A sliding glass wall connects the room with a terrace overlooking the azure bay of Ibiza, Spain. Soft, cotton-covered lounging furniture occupies the juncture between indoors and out, facing the rugged coastline.

▲ **Sliding glass walls** connect the
▶ interior of this beach house with a
terrace, imaginatively designed to
resemble a wooden boardwalk.
Moore Ruble Yudell Architects &
Planners conceived the flexible
walls to accommodate multiple
configurations. Alone, the owner
can relax on the casual wicker sofas
in the light-soaked living room;
when entertaining family on week-
ends, she can throw the walls open
for extra space. Decorating with the
soft colors of the sand and ocean
inside and the seaside grasses on
the deck, the architects created a
sensory connection between the
house and its surroundings.

▲ **The back wall** of this breezy living room slides away to merge the indoor space with a shaded patio. Outdoor-style brick paving connects the two spaces and a colorfully clad, built-in daybed seamlessly continues the sitting area onto the patio. Inside, a woven rattan colonial easy chair introduces a romantic element of the tropics. Fresh slip-covered sofas and palm-printed pillows carry the motif.

▶ **In place of one wall,** this living room uses a folding shutter. When closed, the wooden panels keep out insects while still admitting the fragrant ocean air off the coast of Cabo San Lucas, Mexico. Here, the open doorway invites the swimming pool and Pacific Ocean into the room. The blue-checkered rug and blue cushions on the wicker chairs echo the cool water outside, connecting the three layers of space.

The arched doorway of this dining room leads straight out to the veranda. In the warm tropical climate of Bali, Indonesia, there is no need for a door. The dining set, by Bali-based manufacturer Warisan, is hand-hewn from reclaimed teak to add a textured, rustic character. An antique painted cabinet is used as a sideboard, supporting a bountiful arrangement of tropical flowers and palm fronds.

Dense jungles surround this wide-open living room based on the traditional architecture of the tropical Southeast Asian islands. Crooked ironwood tree trunks, which were once used as electricity poles, now help to brace the living room's high thatched ceiling, bringing the forest inside the lavish living space. Colorful cushions, made from the fabric used for monks' robes in Thailand, line deep, carved teak sofas and form soft seats alongside the woven coffee table.

A serene interior courtyard is the focal point of this warm yet minimal house. Kanner Architects created a space that literally opens itself to the outside through operable glass walls that fold and slide into the house, removing barriers between residents and the horizon. Nowhere is this feature more striking than in the home's bathroom, where the glazed wall in front of the deep soaking tub slides away on metal tracks, connecting the tub to the pool that runs parallel beyond the wall. This emphasis on water has a cooling effect and provides emotional inspiration for the owner.

▲ **The owner of this house,** a
◄ German entrepreneur, moved to
Brazil for its tropical sunlight and
stunning beaches. Architect
Claudio Bernardes gives him a
glass house, using curtain walls to
expose the urban Rio de Janeiro
residence to natural light and
ocean views. On the downstairs
level, pivoting glass panels take
the place of walls, admitting cool
ocean breezes. In the master bedroom, sliding glass doors and
walls provide views of the coastline and sunlight surges through
vaulted skylights.

Finding Fresh Air

Patios, porches, decks, and terraces are popular extensions to homes worldwide—a testament to just how much we value those paved and covered spaces just outside the house. These are some of the most accessible forms of outdoor rooms, available on sprawling country estates or tight suburban lots. By simply adding the right combination of furniture, accessories, and plants to these preexisting planes, owners can experience a relaxing retreat just outside their door. Bounded by the house, yet potentially worlds away, these spaces exemplify our ability to enjoy the visceral experience of nature and the comfortable sensation of the indoors at the same time.

▶ **Placed beneath the shelter** of a covered porch, this elegantly furnished glass-top dining table is placed to overlook the Caribbean Sea—a view framed by sculptural flowering trees. The atmosphere on the porch reflects the glamour of its surroundings. Fresh fruits and flowers and brightly painted china adorn the delicately shaped wrought iron table. Underfoot, a polished slate floor gives the space a dramatic feel.

◀ **Bright shades of green and blue** create a tropical atmosphere on this spacious patio. A low stone wall and thatched pavilions break the expanse into intimate rooms for lounging and dining. Oversized stone planters introduce abundant greenery, which helps to screen a private sitting area.

Porches

Porches have been an integral part of architecture for hundreds of years. The mere mention of a porch conjures images of a lazy summer afternoon, sipping ice-cold lemonade during a leisurely siesta in a wicker easy chair. A versatile outdoor room sheltered beneath the extending roofline of the house, a porch can be easily redefined through furniture and accessories. As such, it lends itself to many variations and styles.

◄ **A wicker dining set** provides a comfortable spot for a morning cup of coffee. Potted plants displayed on the woven tabletop and a tiered garden shelf echo the abundance of greenery visible beyond the porch's carved wood beams. Bamboo shades blend in with the natural setting and can be lowered for shade and privacy.

▶ **Pink walls and palm trees** augment the tropical ambiance on this Harbor Island, Bahamas, porch. A ceiling fan and smooth tile floor balance the verdant outdoor environment with comfortable indoor-style trappings. Scrolling whitewashed furniture, softened by pink floral cushions, adds a romantic touch to the sitting area, where sculpted metal fish play on the wall.

▲ **Piles of pillows** decorate a deep, leopard-cloaked daybed on this cozy porch. The assortment of color and pattern creates layers of visual texture against the house's neutral clapboard siding. Unmatched accessories, such as the stack of books, flea market lamp, black medallion, and wicker side chair, achieve a studied casual look.

◄ **Wooden rockers** embody the ideal of a traditional porch, where families sit into the evening telling stories as crickets chirp in the distance. This Michigan porch captures the old-fashioned image with unfinished wood columns and a simple arrangement of matching rocking chairs that looks out onto a wooded setting.

▲ **A long wooden bench** is well
suited to this narrow porch.
Flowering vines climb the white
columns, sheltering the small
space from the nearby residences
in this urban area. Potted plants
add color along the quaint rails of
the wooden banister.

▲ **This porch,** belonging to the owner of Bali-based furniture company Warisan, is decorated with some of his most popular teak easy chairs. Their square, contemporary lines contrast with the tangle of tropical greenery that grows beneath the elevated concrete platform. A carved wooden trellis adds shade and highlights a popular local craft.

◄ **This farmhouse** outside Cape Town, South Africa, blends African and European influences. A natural cane awning protects the veranda, where cushioned cane furniture creates a comfortable sitting area around a coffee table made from planks of found wood. Throw pillows introduce the colors of the sunset and accessories like the African drum add local flavor. A wooden bench sits at the edge of the veranda, where the farmers can soak up inspirational views of the countryside.

▲ **This loggia blends** Islamic and European influences. The detailed molding of the arches is borrowed from Arabian loggias, but the furnishings are more American style. The wicker armchairs and ottomans are woven to resemble overstuffed living room furniture. Topiaries in stone pots introduce a classical element.

▶ **A crisp palate** of white and navy blue gives a nautical flavor to this oceanfront porch. Its whitewashed wooden railing and old-fashioned metal lantern have a historic quality, but the simple, clean arrangement of the wicker easy chairs adds contemporary finesse.

▲ **The loggia originated** in the warm
climate of ancient Egypt and its
arched colonnades suggest exotic
Arabian style. Color abounds on
this ornate loggia in Marrakech,
Morocco, which faces a tiled garden courtyard. Columns and walls
are accented with molded terra-
cotta details and blue and white
mosaic tiles. Sunlight filters through
the palms in the garden, softly
illuminating a carved wooden
bench draped in rich fabrics.

Patios

Bright and bold or simple and serene, patios provide a well-defined paved surface on which to relax and entertain friends and family. Often located between the house and a larger yard, the patio is a transitional space where one can experience the great outdoors without venturing too far into it.

▶ **The owner of this modern** yet
◀ playful patio wanted a space that
reflected his love of Hollywood
and the movies. Architect Aleks
Istanbullu uses brightly colored
stucco walls to infuse the patio
with energy. The cloverleaf swimming pool—reputedly a set piece
for swimming champion and MGM
film star Esther Williams—is a
whimsical centerpiece that dates
back to the 1950s. Guests can
gather poolside beneath palm-
thatched pavilions to sip on marti-
nis while the host barbeques
nearby. Seats at the casual wooden
dining table or the stone-encircled
fire pit afford views of the
Hollywood Hills.

▲ **Bold color** and polished surfaces give a sleek, contemporary feel to this two-level patio. A fireplace punched into the black stucco wall holds a pile of neatly stacked logs. Bright orange upholstered chairs create bold focal points, while a built-in banquet provides extra seating without interrupting the minimal aesthetic.

▶ **As avid outdoor living fans,** the owners of this home wanted a backyard with spaces for entertaining and relaxing that did not detract from the rustic style of their California ranch house. Designer Gary Orr responded with a wide slate-paved patio surrounding the built-in pool. Furnishings are downplayed to emphasize the patio's long trellis supporting the owner's collection of climbing vines.

Set amid a grove of tall trees and nestled against a towering brick manor, this patio maintains a sense of intimacy and exudes an aged patina. Carefully chosen details achieve classical style. An iron bull's head fountain trickles musically into a stone basin beneath a vine-covered trellis. Weathered teak chairs are adorned with scrolled arms and flaring legs.

An arched trellis supports the owner's prized collection of climbing roses and vines, contributing to the comfortable, old California ranch ambiance crafted by designer Gary Orr. Custom lighting fixtures cast soft pools of illumination, creating the perfect setting for a wrought iron bench. The rustic slate flooring extends to the pool area, where a wooden table and chairs sit on a quiet dining patio warmed by a brick fireplace.

Lush layers of ferns, palms, and potted plants take the place of walls in this open-air living room. Plump, colorful pillows create a comfortable seat on the carved, wood-frame sofa. A grouping of well-used candles provides soft ambient light in the evenings, but for now, patches of sunlight filter in through the verdant leaves.

Rustic furnishings and vivid splashes of color give this patio a spicy Mexican flavor. Bright blue window panes stand out dramatically against the home's earth-colored stucco walls and red flowers burst from terra-cotta pots. Oversized lounging furniture, handmade from aged wood, is softened by white cushions and placed under the shade of an overhang delineated by unfinished wood beams. Hanging from one of the rough support columns, a bundle of dried chili peppers and an aged jug add the finishing touches.

Traveling through a lush garden of native plants, a brick path leads up to this Southwestern-style covered patio. Its built-in corner fireplace, accented by embedded ceramic tiles and a mounted buffalo skull, is the focal point for the outdoor room. Rustic clay pots decorate its wide hearth and a wooden bench sits nearby to soak up the heat.

A small area behind this traditional home is transformed into a cozy outdoor living room, perfect for entertaining guests. A sisal rug frames a conversation area in front of the whitewashed fireplace. Throw pillows, cushions and blankets make comfortable seats on wood and metal furniture whose mismatched qualities create a relaxed atmosphere. The use of neutral colors ties the pieces together into a cohesive and elegant room. A striped awning adds intimacy to the space, and tall citrus trees and potted plants are placed in front of the windows to create a world apart from the inside of the house.

Designer Sheldon Harte brings this fireside outdoor room to life with bright citrus tones. Sleek, lime-green cushions cover two wooden love seats, whose bases are carved in a florid relief. A light orange cushion provides an extra seat on the matching ottoman. The lounging area is shaded by a trellis, draped with vines that sway in the wind and cast dancing shadows across the deep patio.

▶ **Tall potted plants** mitigate the rigid lines of this Zurich home's contemporary architecture, giving the patio a relaxed, natural atmosphere. A wooden lounger casts a dramatic reflection in the still waters of the patio's shallow pond, illuminated by soft light from rusted, candle-lit lanterns. Despite its strict, clean-lined border, the pond maintains a natural appearance with lily pads floating lazily on its surface and cattails softening its edges.

▲ **Artist Kharlene Boxenbaum** and her husband enjoy relaxing on the back patio of their contemporary Los Angeles home. Architect Steven Ehrlich separates this long space into two intimate rooms with a looming stucco wall panel that extends from the house.

▶ **Two metal lounge chairs** sit outside the library that overlooks a slope planted with shrubs. On the dining patio, a long, polished counter reaches out to hover over the garden. This minimalist aesthetic emphasizes the natural setting and maintains a serene, meditative environment.

◀ **Lush landscaping** brings untamed life onto this small, stone-paved patio. A twisted tree branch provides a natural canopy, while colorful flowers attract butterflies and hummingbirds. Rough stone walls add texture and depth to the surrounding garden and blend seamlessly into the patio's surface, where small chairs and bistro tables diverge from the natural setting with metallic sheen.

▲ **Rich textures** give an organic touch to this deep covered patio. Sisal mats add a coarse grain beneath the comfortable lounging furniture, which is woven from natural cane and rattan and cushioned in soothing earth tones. Accessories, from the spiraling basket that serves as a side table to the carved lamp and colorful sculpture behind the sofa, have a handmade look that contributes to the patio's eclectic character. Beyond its pillars, nature erupts in textured layers of green.

Decks and Terraces

Decks and terraces expand living space by bridging uneven surfaces, such as the edge of a hill or the roof of a house, with flat, usable planes. The natural wood frame of a deck brings an organic element to any space and conveys the casual, relaxing qualities of the outdoors. Terraces, because of their height, often have the advantage of dramatic, far-reaching views. They are also more exposed to the elements. In some spaces, canopies, transparent walls, and plants provide protection from the sun and wind. Other terraces welcome these invigorating elements.

▶ **This crisp, colorful deck** designe[d] by Shubin + Donaldson Architect[s] links indoors and out with its glas[s] wall. Inside, natural light illumi-nates a master bedroom reading couch. Outside, white fabric flut-ters seductively in the ocean breeze and shelters two cushion-covered loungers—front row seat[s] for viewing the sunset over the Pacific Ocean. Pots of fuzzy catta[il] soften the clean-lined space.

A cheerful candy-striped awning creates a playful impression on the deck of architect Andy Neumann's California beach home. Neumann adds more color to the weathered boards of the deck with bright red geraniums, painted Adirondack chairs, and colorful ceramic pots. Wide expanses of protective glass frame the panoramic ocean views.

▶ **Existing trees** are incorporated into the structure of this deck, which covers an uneven, rocky terrain to provide space for an outdoor living room. Wide cushioned sofas and wicker easy chairs form a conversation area around a weathered wooden coffee table. Large granite boulders, covered in moss and morning glories, form the room's walls and a spanning white umbrella serves as a ceiling.

Elegant curves add sophistication to this wraparound terrace built into a rocky slope in Scottsdale, Arizona. A rounded infinity-edge pool spills over the hillside, defying the boundary created by the row of classical columns. Builder Kitchell Custom Homes and architect Mark Fredstrom incorporated distinctive red boulders from the surrounding hillside into its design, tying the pool to the desert landscape. Along the terrace, different seating arrangements composed of shapely sofas, easy chairs, and pillows in bright colors break the long space into a series of intimate living rooms.

Elevated high above the roar of the city, this urban terrace is a secluded retreat where traffic noise is muffled by the sound of the wind rustling through potted plants. Two teak loungers provide an inspiring vantage point of the bay beyond the high-rise buildings. In a separate dining area, plump pillows and elegant table settings bring out the luxuries of the indoors. Sensuously spiraling shells placed on every plate connect the terrace to its ocean setting.

Dining Out

As people migrate toward the outdoors, the activities they used to conduct indoors move with them. The emergence of elaborate outdoor kitchens and dining spaces proves the point. Gone are the days of the grimy grill, paper plates, and plastic forks. Today's outdoor gourmets command luxury cooking stations with amenities aimed at convenient, precise food preparation. Of course, a good meal requires a great al fresco setting in which to enjoy it. Many outdoor kitchens are accompanied by lavish dining areas that enhance the pleasure of eating in the open air, where everything tastes better and life is one long picnic.

Designer Gary Orr created this Zenlike patio offset by a colonnade of stucco columns draped luxuriously with passion vines. Small trees define the outdoor room, while seasonal plantings spill from ceramic pots, filling the space with their sweet aromas. A rock-bottom reflecting pool mirrors a sensuous canopy of draping cloth before morphing seamlessly into a polished concrete dining table. Cushioned benches parallel the table for extra seating. A series of intimate rooms fills the garden space—a cooking nook, a sitting terrace, an eight-seat spa, and a fireplace gathering area.

Outdoor Kitchens

Today's outdoor kitchens dissolve the boundaries between work and play. Amenities such as built-in barbeques, smoker ovens, cabinet and counter space, sinks, and bars make cooking and entertaining a pleasure. From their fully outfitted command posts, chefs can revel in mountain, ocean, and poolside views. Lounging in nearby dining nooks, family and friends are never far from the grill.

◄ **Brightly painted** cabinet doors and counter tiles define this outdoor kitchen, nestled in the corner of a country-style covered patio. Colored task lighting hangs from rough wood beams overhead. In the dining area, settings reflect the outdoor location—organic place-mats made from bound twigs, a heavy clay pot, and an elaborate, rusted chandelier hanging from the vaulted, wood-beam ceiling. Forming a partial wall is a rustic brick fireplace, beyond which diners can view a leafy garden.

In this sanctuary for outdoor dining, a built-in barbeque offset by ornamental masonry takes center stage. The tiled counter and bank of cabinets provide the cook with space for prep work. Diners can kick back in comfortable oversized wicker chairs. Seated at the bar—a built-in counter over the patio's brick edging—they can look out across a desert landscape through wide, arched openings.

▲ **French doors open up** onto this
charming brick-paved dining
patio. Architect William Hefner
uses a low brick wall to define an
outdoor kitchen, equipped with a
gas burner, without separating it
from the wooden dining table. A
trellis shades the patio with mature
vines that dangle from its beams.

▲ **A stainless steel gas barbeque** is built into a countertop on this covered deck. Cherry wood cabinets provide storage space for cooking utensils. Overhead, a built-in hood draws up the smoke from the grill to keep it from overpowering the scent of the crisp ocean air.

◄ **After dinner,** the owners can lounge on comfortable wooden furniture as they savor a glass of wine. A large stone fireplace wards off the chill of ocean breezes along the cool Santa Barbara coast.

Outdoor Dining Rooms

In outdoor dining rooms, the atmosphere around the table is just as important as the food on top of it. Tucked into a covered patio, these spaces have an intimate feel; arranged on a terrace or rooftop, they take advantage of views that inspire the mind as well as the appetite. Elements of the outdoors are incorporated into the dining experience through sights, sounds, and even the textures on the tabletop. Natural wood, linens, and earthenware add an organic touch, while ephemeral crystals and candles create moods through light.

▶ **Architect Conchita Kien** could not bear to cut down several twisted old trees to build a new home, so she let them grow through this long Balinese veranda. In one corner, a glamorous table and chairs covered in mirrored mosaic sit between the veranda's Ethiopian-style polished concrete columns that gleam like marble, overlooking the island's tropical vegetation. Silver and glass table settings contribute to the airy atmosphere. In another area, a rustic wooden dining table, lined with rich wooden chairs and a carved, antique bench, accommodates larger parties in a more organic setting. Here, the wall is stained green for a warmer, more enclosed feeling.

▲ **Sheltered beneath** the rustic beams of a rural Spanish patio, this dining room blends elements of old and new to create an elegant space with a rich sense of antiquity. The eroded adobe fireplace is dressed with a curving candelabrum that mimics the arc of the leaves that grow from the clay pots. A large painting decorates the rough stone wall, its clean geometry and the crisp colors standing out dramatically against the organic surface. The wide, country-style dining table adds to the rustic environment with simple, natural accessories—white sea shells, bamboo candle holders, and richly colored dishes. Soft, textured cushions line a wooden bench, giving it the look of an upholstered sofa.

◀ **A florid chandelier** bathes this sheltered dining patio in soft ambient light. Tableware in spicy red, purple, and yellow adds a contemporary punch to the natural palate of the Mediterranean architecture. Beyond the rustic stone columns, a fountain pool shimmers in candlelight, surrounding the space with its soothing trickle.

▲ **Beyond the molded arches** of
this deep loggia, a thick garden of
palms shelters an elegant dining
area. Colors are subdued, creating
a relaxed atmosphere. Wrought
iron lounging furniture is cushioned in fresh white, and the
wooden dining set holds an elegant collection of candelabra,
china, and amber-hued barware
that suggest indoor-style sophistication. A detailed metal screen
adds visual texture against the
smooth plastered wall.

▼ **A massive stone fireplace** forms a
partial enclosure for this outdoor
dining room, where natural materials create a serene, rustic setting.
Dining chairs formed from unfinished logs provide extra seating
around the weathered picnic table.
Here, table settings in soft shades
of green and brown blend with
the natural setting.

The graceful symmetry of its architecture gives a formal appearance to this clean-lined porch. Cotton slipcovers and a bright, pleated tablecloth bring out the comfort of the indoors, creating an airy spot for a weekend brunch. Potted cattails were carefully chosen for their sculptural qualities that contrast with the bushy wildlife beyond the porch's white columns and swinging gates.

▶ **Interior designer** Lilia Konrad creates a colorful dining vignette on her terrace overlooking Lake Zug in Switzerland. Lime-green glasses sparkle in the early morning sunlight, while mint-colored ceramic bowls blend with the natural tone of the wood table and cushioned folding chairs. An elegant side table provides extra space for colorful accessories and trays of food and drink. Two sculpted topiaries act as columns that anchor the corners of the platform deck.

▶ **Abstract furniture and sculptures** imitate the shapes of the skyline beyond this colorful rooftop terrace. In their private miniature garden city, the owners preside on high-rise thrones of wood and metal as they dine at the top of the world. A chunky concrete table lined with potted plants blends natural and industrial influences. Squares of inlaid wood, stained in a woven color pattern, mimic the effect of area rugs on the deck floor.

◀ **When designing** this traditional Alpine cottage, architect Carlo Rampazzi was inspired by the local Gothic architecture as well as the color and unexpected surprises of surrealist paintings. He incorporates elements of each into this fairytale dining terrace lined with gingerbread carving. Long-legged woven furniture by Dedon has a spiderlike quality. A dwarf citrus tree adds a splash of color in the foreground of the mountain scenery and emanates a delicious aroma.

Tropical elegance defines this elevated dining terrace with inspirational views of Bali's forested hills. Votive candles line the cantilevered stone floor, inches from the precipice, illuminating the view in the setting evening sun. For a romantic touch, sweet-smelling flower petals are sprinkled across the floor and the tabletop, where traditional woven cloths mingle with luxurious, European-style settings.

Light and water add dramatic effects to this rooftop dining room. A row of candles lights the way down the wooden staircase leading to the silver dining table and delicately formed metal chairs, which shimmer in the ephemeral glow of candlelight. An elegant glass water feature pours into a pebble-lined channel, creating a moat around the dining table. Lighting Design International created a built-in scheme that casts halos around the potted trees that line the edge of the space.

This shady courtyard exudes elegant Asian style. Soaring beams of unfinished wood support a translucent canopy, which admits dappled natural light and views of the treetops. Thick floor cushions in soft, soothing colors line the dark wooden dining table, where symmetry prevails in the collection of smooth ceramic dinnerware. Carefully chosen accessories like the glazed pot and bamboo serving cart add eclectic flair. Contrasting with the order at the center of the room, a lush, layered garden screens the courtyard at its perimeter.

Expanding Boundaries

Besides expanding usable living space, courtyards, garden rooms, and pool areas expand the boundaries of the imagination, challenging our very definition of a room. With a piece of open land as their canvas, the designers and homeowners in this chapter play with boundaries and space to create comfortable rooms defined by their contending sensations of openness and intimacy. Furniture, focal points, paving, and plants all conspire to tame nature and bring a livable scale to the outdoors.

The earthy feel of this Moroccan-themed courtyard reflects the dramatic desert landscape beyond its stucco walls. Designer Jerry Beale of Wilson and Associates accompanied the owners on a buying trip to Morocco where they purchased the Persian rugs, lanterns, and accessories that adorn the space. Flashes of vivid blue, inspired by the pottery of the region, add exotic flair to the warm, natural color scheme. Luxurious cushions of silk and cotton line the built-in sunken banquette along the pool's edge.

Courtyards

Surrounded on several sides by walls, courtyards shut out the noise and bustle of the public world while remaining open to the sky above—a perfect mix of privacy and openness. Traditional courtyards, inspired by Mediterranean design, boast lush gardens that block unsightly views and gushing stone fountains that drown out street noises. Contemporary interpretations maintain the idea of a secluded inner sanctum that offers tranquility, even in a busy urban environment.

▲ **A canopy of tall trees** and potted
▶ ferns enshrouds this Argentine courtyard in mystery, creating a new surprise around every leafy corner. Whimsical garden statues peak out from behind the lacy branches, partially hidden in the copse, and a spiral staircase blends almost imperceptibly with the bowed tree trunks. Reflecting the glamorous, European-style sophistication that Argentina is known for, a lace-covered dining table occupies the center of the courtyard. Glass mosaic benches refract the stray beams of light that seep through the treetops, covering the floor with luminous sequins.

◀ **Soft yellow walls** add a warm, intimate feeling to this small court-yard. Comfortable cushioned and sling furniture is gathered around the built-in fountain, which drowns out any noise from beyond the walls. This cool, quiet retreat takes on a radiant glow in the afternoon sunlight that filters through the canopy of trees.

▶ **A reflecting pool** shimmers in the center of this intimate stone-paved courtyard. Lighting designer Randall Whitehead creates texture and drama with a low-voltage lighting system that subtly highlights key decorative elements, such as a lounging statue, colorful pottery, and a wooden bench. Up lighting emphasizes the delicate silhou-ettes of ferns and trees, while down lighting imitates the effect of moonlight washing the garden. A mirror placed on the back wall reflects the light and makes the small space seem bigger.

Designer Thomas Beeton, renowned for his opulent interiors, lends his flair for luxury to this courtyard living room. He arranges an oversized, royal blue wicker sofa and easy chairs around a scrolled mirror-top table, where they can soak up the warmth from the fireplace. Green and white throw pillows coordinate with the sweet-smelling honeysuckle that climbs the garden walls. Underfoot, stone pavers overgrown with clover form a geometric yet natural rug.

▶ **A rough wooden table** carved from a log holds a sumptuous morning snack in this Spanish courtyard. The imperfections in the wood form a natural accent to the leafy space and contrast with the polished lines of the sleek folding chair. This cozy dining room occupies only a small part of the walled-off room. The remaining space is given to a wide, sloping stretch of garden whose colorful geraniums, palms, and clay pots form a buffer between the peaceful courtyard and the rooftops of the surrounding neighborhood.

◀ **To update the grounds** of a 1920s Mediterranean estate in southern California, landscape architect Katherine Spitz uses brick paving and tile mosaics. An arabesque-shaped fountain occupies the center of the courtyard, fed by a steam of water running from a low tiled wall. Mission-style furniture in heavy wood and leather is placed to complement the serene space from a brick patio.

▲ **A staggered brick wall** is the foundation for the pueblo-style architecture that creates a Southwestern feeling in this colorful courtyard. Glazed flowerpots and tiles in bold red, orange, green, and blue bring the space to life and introduce a regional palate. At the wrought iron dining table, an umbrella offers protection from the harsh sun, while a built-in beehive fireplace wards off the evening chill.

▲ **Architect Richard Corsini** uses a billowing fiberglass-mesh canopy and curtain to provide a soft counterpoint to the contemporary hardscape of this courtyard. He places deep, cushioned loungers on a concrete platform beneath the canopy, where they are protected from the sun to the southwest.

◄ **A built-in concrete bench** surrounds the wide, sunken fire pit. This area is lined in river rock made from the home's driveway, which was demolished to make room for the new space. Lean, sculptural plantings add color and privacy, as does the red stucco wall framing the back of the courtyard.

▲ **Combining metal,** modern furniture, and clean-lined plantings, British landscape designer Courseworks and automaker Mitsubishi team up to create a sophisticated, urban chic courtyard for England's Hampton Court garden show. Metallic balls form shiny bubbles on the surface of a black pool. On the surrounding deck, curving lounge chairs sit on a platform striped with aluminum. Creating a pattern across the floor, gaps in the decking are filled in with gravel and fragrant thyme.

▶ **This compact entry courtyard**
▽ provides a colorful haven only a
few feet off the suburban street.
Landscape architect Katherine
Spitz separates the room with a
wall of bamboo and fragrant
pomegranate and persimmon
trees. A concrete path approaches
the home's front door, weaving
through a geometric collage of
gravel, redwood, water, and native
plantings. Colored glass panels
disperse sunlight over reflecting
pools and add an extra layer of privacy. The owner, a West Hollywood
urban planner, revels in the environment from a wide redwood
bench in the center of the garden.

A periwinkle blue wall blocks unsightly views and creates a lively atmosphere inside this decked dining courtyard. Aqua-painted wooden dining chairs complement the blue tile mosaic tabletop, where a tall bouquet of wildflowers stands out dramatically against the solid backdrop. By limiting the number of colors in the space, the owners keep the bright palette from becoming overwhelming.

▲ **Professors Andrew and Karla** Newell erected solid, bright blue walls to give this cozy, latticed corner a greater sense of enclosure. The painted and tiled walls transform the stone-paved urban courtyard into a charming teahouse, where red and orange pillows add warm blocks of color along the banquette, which is formed by contoured benches along the slatted wooden tea table. Potted plants outline a grand entryway and a vine-covered timber pergola shelters the space from the high-rise buildings outside.

Garden Rooms

Nestled in foliage, these dynamic spaces straddle the delicate balance between wilderness and civilization. Man-made comforts, from picnic tables and fireplaces to sofas and even beds, can be arranged to create the cozy illusion of a room, but it is ultimately the element of wilderness that defines the garden room experience. Rays of sunlight awaken the senses, wind rustles through the trees, and new flowers blossom every day.

Using an organic palette of natural stone and dense plantings, landscape architect Scott Daigre turns a long, sloping run of grass into a series of garden rooms with an instant sense of age. Different spaces unfold, each more secluded than the last, as one follows the winding stone path through the garden. A sunny lawn used for entertaining morphs into a curving nook with a built-in fire pit and rounded banquette.

Suspended over the hillside on the rugged Big Sur coastline, this simple deck floats like an island amid a lush garden of bushes and native flowering plants. Without a railing, its blue-gray boards blend in with the distant Pacific Ocean. Metal garden chairs have curving arms that mimic the shape of the bay.

▲ **Recycled materials** add whimsical charm to this shady garden room. Old doors are reclaimed and painted in bright colors to form a backdrop for the room's center-piece—a wooden platform daybed lined in casual cotton pillows. Glass bottles are placed upside down on rebar poles to form flowers that bloom all year long.

Rios Clementi Hale Studios designed several intimate areas within this expansive garden. A wall of hedges and a trellis of bamboo and cedar posts define a Moroccan- themed outdoor living room, where the concrete-tile floor is designed to resemble a Tibetan carpet. Moroccan lanterns hang from the trellis, illuminating the sitting area furnished with Sunbrella-cushioned wrought iron furniture. Beyond the living room are a Japanese-style water garden and a dining area, defined by bluestone pavers overgrown with creeping thyme and chamomile. A bright yellow dining table by Roy McMakin is a vibrant focal point.

◀ **Taking advantage** of a steep hillside, ORR Design Office created a lush, Northern Italian–style garden park. A grand staircase, gently illuminated by post lamps and lined with edge plantings of Juniper and dwarf oleander, connects the top of the hillside with the bottom.

▶ **A round dining terrace** occupies the top level. Below, a gurgling fountain beckons, filled with water plantings and goldfish. Large clay pots of citrus trees and herbs envelop the garden in their fragrance, and a tall forest of oaks and pines adds an intimate feeling of seclusion.

A combination of organic textures and feminine details creates a "shabby chic" effect in this garden alcove. Weathered stone pavers add warmth and a sense of age, while the details in the furnishings are light and airy—a refreshing complement to the sweet-smelling white roses beyond the sheltered room. The intricate metalwork of the trellis echoes the curves of the climbing vines that wind their way into the room. On the wall, an ornate beveled mirror shimmers like a diamond. The overall effect is one of casual elegance.

▼ **A gravel platform** extends this informal dining area into the garden, where shapely aloe and ice plants cover the ground in a twisting carpet. Marmol Radziner + Associates cover the wall of an outbuilding with a thick blanket of climbing vines to hide the residential structure, allowing diners to enjoy a picnic in the middle of nature.

▲ **Fanciful sculpture** gives character
to this peaceful San Francisco garden room, designed by Keela
Meadows. A molded copper morning glory arch leads the way onto
the brick path, which wanders
through dense plantings of yellow
tulips. Bright purple and blue
retaining walls hold deep planters
full of wildflowers. In a quiet alcove,
a colorful butterfly bench provides
a place for enjoyment.

▼ **A wood-fired** cedar hot tub
invites deep relaxation in the natural setting of this lush garden
room. Designer Paul Herrington
leaves a wide variety of plants to
grow on their natural course,
creating a woodlike setting. Logs,
eventually used as fuel for the hot
tub, are stacked into a retaining
wall that keeps the plants off the
spiraling pebble mosaic path leading up to the deep, barrel-like tub.

Pool Surrounds

Many of the world's greatest civilizations have evolved around water. Why not an outdoor room, as well? When the swimming pool is the center of life, it makes sense to create a space where you can enjoy lounging, dining, and warmth without straying too far from the water's edge. Using sumptuous furnishings and carefully engineered areas of heat and shade, these spaces take pool surrounds to a new level of luxury.

▼ **A waterfall pours** over the bright blue retaining wall that encloses this sunken pool surround. The small, hidden area offers many comfortable options for exercise and relaxation. After a refreshing swim, the owners can retreat onto a wide canopied bed or gather around a wooden table at the cushioned banquette. Blue-glazed pots and an assortment of pillows in many shapes, sizes, and colors infuse the space with liveliness.

▲ **Several lounging and dining** spaces follow the curving shore of this long infinity-edge swimming pool, creating a private resort overlooking the Pacific Ocean. Sheltered by tropical palm fronds, a dramatically grained wooden dining table is surrounded by wide, cushioned wicker chairs. From groupings of wooden loungers and easy chairs, the owners can watch the sailboats drift across the waves.

Using cool glass, Katherine Spitz creates a refreshing poolside retreat in southern California's warm San Fernando Valley. Blue glass tiles shimmer at the bottom of the traditional rectangular swimming pool. At one end of the pool, these icy tiles enclose the round spa; at the other end they form a backdrop for a waterfall. Modern glass tables are positioned in shaded alcoves with playful white plastic bar stools. Adding warmth to the clean, contemporary lines of the space is a glowing fireplace with a built-in bench.

▲ **A built-in fireplace** and a long
rectangular dining table transform this narrow passageway into
a cozy room overlooking the
swimming pool. Marmol Radziner
+ Associates designed and fabri-
cated the outdoor furniture without ornamentation, letting the
swirling grains of its wood planks
create a connection to the lush
landscape. Tall bushes form walls
around two sides of the swimming
pool, enclosing the space and
softening the geometrical hardscape of concrete pavers. The
cool earth tones of blue, gray, and
brown blend with the greenery to
create a relaxing atmosphere.

► **Narrowing to a cool inlet,** this sparkling Indonesian swimming pool extends beneath a covered patio, where soft colors and organic materials add a deep feeling of refreshment. An upholstered lounger, accented with textured rattan, provides a comfortable seat for reading. On the pool's opposite bank, a sensuously curving chaise draws attention to the natural quality of its wood. Pieces of found wood with a visibly cracked grain form a striking wall sculpture above.

◄ **Using a natural stone** surface, Rios Clementi Hale Studios places a long, luxurious pool in the corner of this hedged garden. Here, swimming is an act of quiet meditation. Wooden lounge chairs sit on a patch of moss shaded by white umbrellas and tall trees. At the corner of the pool surround, a hollow stone post holds a dancing fire that emits a gentle glow for a relaxing nighttime dip.

▲ **Landscape designer** Rios
Clementi Hale Studios creates a
contemporary outdoor living room
centered on a shimmering black-
bottom swimming pool. A richly
colored ironwood deck holds sleek
metal lounge chairs and planters
of colorful native flora—a soothing, clean-lined space to bask in
the sun. The warm ironwood
reaches into the indoor pool room,
where it meets flush with a cool
terrazzo floor, forming a bridge
between indoors and out. Floor-
to-ceiling sliding glass doors connect the comfortable pool room,
with its modern artwork and
upholstered banquettes, to the
pool outside.

Taking Shelter

These protective outdoor structures balance impressions of enclosure and openness, offering shelter without shutting you inside. Their walls, whether made from plants, glass, or simply a tenuous illusion created by a few beams, enclose a piece of the outdoors. Positioned outside the house, they offer an escape from daily life and chance to experiment in style. Some of these outdoor rooms imitate the formal styles of English garden houses or Greek pavilions; others are more playful in appearance.

▶ **Self-taught designers** Ilga Jansons
▲ and Mike Dryfoos created a lush Asian-style koi garden on their wooded Seattle property. A large joglo structure—a tall, open pavilion that Ilga and Mike collected during a trip to Indonesia—anchors the diverse garden of Douglas fir, cedar, fern, azalea, and wide-leaved tropical plants. Under its shingled roof, one can sit on cushioned folding chairs and watch the large koi flashing in the dark pond outside.

Tree House Retreats

The ultimate outdoor escape, a tree house stirs images of adventure. For a child, they provide a space to form secret clubs or hide from pirates. For adults, tree houses offer new opportunities for quiet rest and relaxation, far from the electronic drone of the computer and fax machine. Many grown-ups have brought their fantasies to life in innovative and sophisticated playhouses that offer an escape from the serious side of life.

A series of stairs and platforms lead a grand procession up to the terraced entrance, perched 24 feet (7.3 m) in the air. Supported by metal cables, the cedar-clad tree house sways gently in the breeze. Operable casement windows light the room and provide communion with the outdoors.

The owner of this tree house, a busy advertising executive, wanted a private retreat where he could escape the pressures of the business day and play with his two sons. He called on architects McIntosh Poris Associates to build a tree house on his wooded property in Detroit, Michigan.

▲ **A sprawling,** multi-room tree house overlooks the quiet woodland scenery outside Seattle. Designers Ilga Jansons and Mike Dryfoos leave the walls open except for the support beams and railings, admitting greenery and natural light into every corner. Comfortable furnishings promote relaxation in the secluded retreat. In this nook, a bed is piled with throw pillows and draped with a luxurious jewel-toned comforter.

▶ **This country cottage** in the trees makes a romantic retreat, perfect for an afternoon tea or a cozy chat. An ascent through the foliage on a simple staircase lined with potted plants leads to the idyllic French doors, which are painted in a soft, weathered green to add warmth and richness. Open just a crack, they invite the smell of roses into the space that is inevitably filled with floral fabrics and rich woods.

Gazebos and Pavilions

Often used as a decorative focal point in the garden, gazebos and pavilions also provide a sheltered space in which to relax. Some embrace the outdoors, offering a minimal enclosure of columns or latticework. Others are fully enclosed and their walls harbor decadent living and dining rooms with garden views.

◄ **Jim Reynolds' Butterstream** garden, situated along a creek in the Irish countryside, is a labor of love that has been perfected over more than twenty years. Reynolds incorporates intimate rooms that act as focal points and provide sheltered spaces from which to enjoy his creation. Here, tall pillars add classical elegance to a weathered green pavilion that blends in with the landscape. A flowering bush climbs to the trellis roof, its fragrant yellow flowers perfuming the air. Inside, a solitary white scrolled bench adds to the space's simple charm.

▲ **A sectional wicker sofa** takes advantage of this cozy corner to form a sitting room with a spectacular view inside a sheltered wooden gazebo. Plush pillows and a sisal rug bring out the comforts of the indoors, while a gracefully contoured chandelier holds a ring of burning tapers—a distinctive outdoor luxury.

▶ **The furnishings** inside this formal, glass-enclosed gazebo reflect its garden setting. Bouquets of fruits and flowers are laid across the dining table, draped in a lacy floral cloth, and white metal chairs are padded with rose-print cushions. Sunlight filters through the cloth ceiling, sparkling in the crystal barware.

▲ **Two white gazebos,** their roofs
▶ rising in dramatic spires, frame a
grand stairway entry into the garden at the home of landscape
designer Katherine Spitz and
architect Daniel Rhodes. These
unique and architecturally
detailed structures provide extra
space for a potting shed. Their
translucent polycarbonate roofs
cause the gazebos to glow from
within at night.

▲ **Incorporating formal** architectural
details, this glass-enclosed pavilion, designed by Town and
Country Conservatories, occupies
a stately presence in the prim garden. Decorative finials and ridges
line the stepped, zinc-clad roof
and gable. Curved tracery glazing
gives the summerhouse a delicate,
airy appearance.

Climbing vines shelter this arched wooden gazebo, blocking views of the outside world to create a secluded retreat. Their leaves drape down to tickle the top of the metal dining table where an elegant glass pitcher serves refreshing drinks on a silver platter. Garden chairs with spiraling metal arms add another decadent flourish, while the crushed gravel floor grounds the space with a natural surface.

The wooden beams of this gazebo intertwine indistinguishably with the surrounding tree branches, creating an unassuming natural shelter. Flagstone pavers and a mixed assortment of potted plants define the shady room below, where cushioned metal chairs surround a dining table. The colorful pillows, candles, and tablecloth stand out amid the thick foliage.

Taking a siesta in this thatched Mexican hut, you can listen to the sea breeze play in its palapa roof. The woven hammock, a local specialty, is suspended from the pavilion's natural cane frame, providing a comfortable vantage point over the Sea of Cortez.

This intricately molded Moroccan gazebo by designer Ursula Haldimann and architect Björn Conerdings houses a curving, cushioned banquet where guests relax over tea as they enjoy the lavish courtyard outside. A high, arched doorway allows unobstructed views of lanterns lighting the tiled pathway and a stone pool sprinkled with pink rose petals for romantic allure.

An arched trellis creates a shaded dining room in the Paris garden of fashion designer Hubert James Taffin de Givenchy—the man whose elegant, sophisticated style shaped iconic women such as Audrey Hepburn and Jackie Kennedy. Givenchy's classically-inspired style is evident in clean, easy furnishings, from the natural granite tabletop that rests on antique pillars to the simple but striking arrangement of white-cushioned metal chairs among the white rose bushes.

Trellises

Trellises provide the most minimal type of enclosure. Only their shapes and the shadows they cast define the room below. Left unadorned, the raw beams of a trellis stand out as a stark landmark. Dressed with soft furniture and lush plants, they can be transformed into sumptuous open-air rooms.

▲ **A garden of climbing vines,** trees,
▶ and rose bushes encloses this
casual outdoor living room
designed by architect William
Hefner to accommodate entertaining long into the evening.
During the day, a wide wooden
trellis shelters the space from the
sun. At night, lanterns illuminate
the conversation area. The freestanding stucco fireplace mimics
the architecture of the adjacent
house and the detailed metalwork
of the mirror hanging above its
mantle adds to the Mediterranean
style of the property.

▲ **This rough timber trellis** stands out sculpturally against the azure ocean and sky. Shaded beneath the striped shadows of its beams, a rustic wooden swing overlooks the long swimming pool that stretches out toward the surf.

Twentieth-century novelist and scholar John Erskine once said, "I have never had so many good ideas day after day as when I worked in the garden." The owner of this quiet garden office, defined by a narrow trellis, obviously agrees. Here, minimal furnishings give prominence to the natural setting. The scrolled pink desk chair stands out in the garden like a beautiful rose. On the wooden writing table, a small topiary stands as a muse. Thick, twisting vines climb the trellis walls and trees form a canopy overhead. Stained glass panels provide additional privacy while still admitting fresh natural light.

Two inviting wicker chairs rest in the shade cast by this leafy trellis. Draped in blankets and dappled with sunlight, they suggest leisurely afternoons lost in a good book. The small occasional table between them supports books, drinks, and a colorful bouquet— trimmings that enhance the impression of a complete room. A "carpet" of cement further defines the outdoor room, using natural stone borders and mosaics to create a textured pattern.

Pool Houses

Though they serve a practical purpose, pool houses are about more than just keeping wet feet off the Oriental rug indoors. These gracious poolside structures provide a relaxed environment for drying off slowly in the breeze after a leisurely swim or entertaining friends over a candle-lit dinner on a warm evening. Essentially indoors, yet separate from the main house, pool houses provide an opportunity to create a more casual or adventurous atmosphere—a place to practice your decorative whims.

This chic pool house conveys feminine sophistication with crisp colors, languid curves, and sparkling surfaces. A scrolled wooden armchair stands out dramatically against the white fabric wall. The organic pattern of the zebra skin rug complements its curves. On the clean-lined coffee table, a pink bouquet blends in with the bushy leaves that reflect on the lacquered surface. Crystal pendants, dangling from the glass candleholder, disburse rainbows across the room.

Fung + Blatt Architects transformed an existing redwood stable into a contemporary pool house. Only its weathered boards with their deep grooves recall the original building with its dirt lot. Now, a glistening pool fills the space and a floating wooden trellis extends from the pool house to define a shady dining area. Adding on to the home's livable space, the pool house holds a guest room and bathroom with a shower.

▲ **Deep, curving wicker** club chairs are scaled to fill the wide doorway of this airy southern California pool house, taking advantage of sweeping views of the pool and the mountains beyond. Interior designer Michael Berman cushions these shapely loungers in the warm colors of the afternoon sun—a soothing spectrum of red, orange, and yellow. By introducing luxurious details, such as the braided molding around the coffee table or the delicate metalwork of the lantern-style chandelier, he creates a polished atmosphere.

▶ **Perfectly positioned** and amply lit, this rustic Mediterranean-style pool house casts a shimmering reflection on the water's surface. Landscape architect Katherine Spitz sets the retreat in a forest of refreshing palms whose broad leaves shade the house's tile roof. Inside, Spitz achieves an authentic Spanish colonial style with wrought iron light fixtures and identical high-back sofas flanking a wide brick hearth.

◀ **Part pool house and part bed,** this padded structure tucked into the corner of a covered patio is a relaxing retreat. Its wooden platform floor is completely covered by a single, smooth white cushion and plush bolsters form comfortable seats. Wide windows along two sides of the room let in views of the surrounding Indonesian jungle, while the remaining two sides of the room are left completely open, admitting tropical breezes.

Diverse layers of accessories and art seem to fall naturally into place around this cozy pool house. The structure's casual architecture of lattice arches and bamboo siding is contrasted by the dramatic red walls and a gilded Asian mural inside. Contributing to the environment's opulent eclecticism, lanterns in styles ranging from Arts and Crafts to Asian hang from the pool house and the overgrown trellis outside. Potted plants spill from baskets, buckets, and vases, lining every step to the water's edge. Over the roof, a thriving bush forms a thick canopy, adding to the impression that the pool house simply sprouted from the weathered wooden deck.

The massive scale of these formal Greek pavilions adds grandeur to the poolside. A comfortable dining room unfolds beneath the shelter of the high, domed ceiling that reaches above the tops of the surrounding trees. The soft, warm hues of the golden tablecloths and red-cushioned chairs complement the antique look of the Doric stone columns.

Prefabricated Outdoor Rooms

The booming emergence of prefabricated structures is fueled by our need to have a quiet, detached living and working space close to home. These predesigned structures provide "instant" outdoor rooms that can be assembled in a matter of days or even hours.

The owners of this prefabricated outdoor bedroom enjoy sleeping with a view of the trees and stars. Matthew and Maria Salinger of coLAB Studios clad their "Pod" in translucent corrugated fiberglass that acts like a visual sponge, soaking up colors, shadows, and light on both sides of the walls. Part bedroom, part garden, and part meditation patio, the Pod has a raised deck floor that allows the yard to spill continuously into the space. The lawn produces cool air, which is sucked into the glass-walled sleeping area through floor vents, eliminating the need for cooling in the evening.

This prototype for designer David Ballinger's MetroShed is complemented by modern furnishings, including a Le Corbusier chaise lounge, Phillipe Starck furniture, Jackson Pollack artwork, and Tiffany crystal, that match the architecture's simple lines and natural symmetry. The MetroShed makes modern architecture immediately accessible to homeowners. With a sturdy composition of cedar beams, aluminum sliding glass doors, and UV-protected polycarbonate roofing, it remains insulated year round for use as an office or a retreat.

▶ **The Garden Escape** is a compact, light-flooded retreat whose clean-lined red cedar form is at home in the garden. This airy prefabricated room makes an excellent outdoor office. To accommodate the telecommuter, the building can be connected to existing electrical sockets and telephone wires.

Sensuous Essentials

Furniture and décor have been the driving forces in blurring the lines between indoors and out. Luxuries once intended only for the indoors are now available in an endless array of sunproof, waterproof, and moldproof varieties that stand up to year-round outdoor use in fully furnished outdoor kitchens, living rooms, and dining rooms. Sumptuous styles coincide with rich colors and textured natural materials that emphasize the inherent beauty of the outdoors. From deep, comfortable sofas and loungers to small pleasures like outdoor art or teak serving sets, no detail is ignored.

▶ The Jardin Classic collection from **JANUS et Cie** is made from premium plantation-grown teak and marine-grade metals to reflect the individual expressions of each classically inspired piece.

▼ **Warisan's** rugged Mirai Lounger, with large rear wheels and an adjustable back, is made from durable recycled teak, revealing its natural grain and imperfections. The companion stone-topped side table is ideal for holding cold drinks or books.

■ Sights

The sense of sight forms your first impressions. Your use of eye-catching color, pattern, shape, and motion will determine whether your outdoor room gives an impression of relaxed romance or formal finesse. No matter what look you choose, outdoor lighting will add depth to your space and ensure that your sensuous essentials are visible day and night.

▼ CLASSIC

▼ This outdoor chandelier from **Shady Lady Lighting** brings refinement to a covered porch or patio. Light emanates from the Sunbrella shades topping each of the chandelier's curving wrought iron arms.

▼ The dramatic shape of **Lloyd/Flanders'** Centennial Lounger reflects 100 years of tradition. Dark wicker woven in intricate patterns adds to the cushioned chair's colonial character.

▲ Supported atop a sculpted pillar, **Haddonstone's** polished stainless steel Crescent Sundial will add a stately presence to your outdoor room. By casting shadows that expand and retract throughout the day, it will help you enjoy the sun's constant motion.

▶ Artist Henri Matisse's works that underscore the beauty of the female body also inspire **Sutherland's** teak Matisse Dining Armchair designed by John Hutton, now available through fine showrooms. The feminine curve of the chair's back complements the hand-carved female form detailed on its arms.

▶ The metal detailing of the Gothic Trellis from **Town and Country Conservatories** adds visual interest to blank walls.

▼ The sleek, sophisticated, and slightly retro frame of the Echo chair from **Tropitone** features swooping oval arms of durable aluminum. A fabric sling, available in many colors and patterns, provides comfortable seating.

▲ Foscarini's best-selling Havana Collection now has an outdoor edition available through **YLighting.** The long, elegant Havana Outdoor Pendant Lamp is perfect for lighting ample spaces. Its graceful, glowing shape integrates beautifully into garden settings.

▲ Art takes its cue from nature in the organic design of the Oluce Stone Outdoor Lamps available through **YLighting.** These lights may look like garden rocks, but they radiate like gems.

► Well-suited to small spaces, the Romeo Bench by Paolo Rizzatto for **Serralunga** has a compact, playful shape. The confidently curving bench is available in many colors through **The Magazine.**

▲ The Vu Chaise Lounge from **Brown Jordan** exudes urban sophistication through its clean lines and tubular stainless steel frame. A sleek, tailored cushion finishes the look.

▼ CASUAL

▶ The distinctive shape of an Adirondack chair blends with both classical and contemporary settings. This teak Adirondack from **Country Casual** has a comfortable, angled seat with wide arms that support your favorite drink.

▲ Crafted from high-quality teak, the languidly curving Durham Swing from **Country Casual** introduces a relaxed country style where life moves at a leisurely pace and intimate moments can be enjoyed.

◀ The timeless look of the cedar-constructed Nantucket Arbor from the **Nantucket Post Cap Company** will add casual charm to your outdoor room. Its four post caps are available with LED lights to cast a soft gleam on your path.

▶ The pole-mounted cypress Butterfly House from **Charleston Gardens** will bring life to your outdoor room. Drawn by its soft colors, butterflies will flutter in and out of the house's slotted front.

▶ Inspired by the Sears kit houses of the early 1900s, EcoCottages from **Modern Steel International** include a kit of precut, predrilled, and premarked steel pieces that users can assemble on-site using readily available tools. The cozy, 108-square-foot (32.9 sq. m) Cabana model exudes casual charm with architectural trim, painted shutters, and a porch overhang.

▼ Designed for a generation who grew up with color magazines, TV, and movies, wicker furniture from **Maine Cottage** is available in several spicy hues. The Swan Pond Chair, shown in Rosa, has sloping wicker arms and a painted frame that takes the sensuous curve of a swan's neck.

▲ Weatherprint paintings from **Open Air Designs** bring the elegance and prestige of fine art to outdoor settings. A broad collection of water- and UV-proof art includes abstract, landscape, architectural, and global-themed pieces.

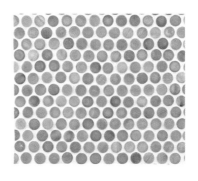

◀ The handmade Glace tile collection from **Ann Sacks** draws inspiration from the luminous qualities of ice. The sparkling iridized glass penny rounds in these tiles—appropriately named Glacier—can shimmer at the base of a fountain or provide a playful backsplash for your outdoor kitchen.

▲ The Buttercup Vine Light from **Nick Williams Designs** features a glass flower on a bendable 6-foot-long (1.8 m) copper vine with detachable leaves. Vine lights will twine around a post, small tree trunk, or through a lattice, adding color and whimsy to your outdoor room.

▶ The Cobalt Conservatory Lamp from **Town and Country Conservatories** features a florid light fixture of blown glass. Its scrolling metal base has tendrils that curl up against the light like leaves.

▶ Lime-green, weather-resistant cushions add a splash of color to the highly geometric steel frame of the Talt Sofa from **Modern Outdoor.** Lounge in luxury on its deep, 33-inch (83.8 cm) seat.

■ Smells and Sounds

Appealing to the often-ignored senses of sound and smell will create a richer experience in your outdoor room. Surround yourself with fragrant flowers and herbs in pots and planters, invite the music of warbling birds, and drown out the noise of everyday life with the relaxing rush of water.

▼ SOUNDS

▶ Designed to be built into any wall, the **Napoleon** Waterfall has a brushed steel back panel covered by a continuous stream of water and illuminated by low-voltage recess lighting.

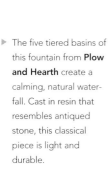

▲ Inspired by the lean, elegant styles of the Art Deco era, **Haddonstone's** Cube Collection features planters with a simple yet distinctive geometry that suits both traditional and contemporary spaces.

▲ An Egg Bird Feeder from the **J. Schatz Collection** attracts many types of birds whose warbling will fill your outdoor room with music. Handmade from glossy ceramic earthenware, its clean design, available in nine colors, blends in with any outdoor environment.

▶ The five tiered basins of this fountain from **Plow and Hearth** create a calming, natural waterfall. Cast in resin that resembles antiqued stone, this classical piece is light and durable.

▲ An oxidized finish adds a natural patina to the handsome Bronzed Vessel Fountain from **Charleston Gardens.** Its gentle trickle creates a soothing backdrop to your outdoor room.

▼ The hand-forged wrought iron Regency Planter from **Charleston Gardens** features elegant scroll-work that suits classical and Mediterranean spaces.

▲ The Mexican Chata Pot imported by **Well Traveled Living** is available in a range of earth tones to create an organic ambiance in your outdoor room.

▼ Scented candles, such as the striped China Pear and Indonesian Teak pillars from **Cost Plus World Market,** offer refreshing aromas that sooth the senses.

▲ A built-in lamp casts a dramatic spotlight on the contents of the Bella Noche Planter from **Shady Lady Lighting.** In an inventive, space-saving design, the classical, urn-style planter holds flora of your choice and also serves as the base for a standing lamp.

▼ Covered with flowers or vines, the Rolling Planter/Trellis from **Plow and Hearth** is a garden as well as a mobile privacy screen.

Textures and Temperatures

Enjoying the new sensations that nature brings against your skin is a distinct part of the outdoor experience. Embrace these adventurous textures with natural materials, from the smooth, deep grains of aged wood to the corrugated ridges of wicker and bamboo. Of course, there is no need to "rough it" in an outdoor room. Bring out the comforts of the indoors with soft fabrics and cushions and keep extreme temperatures at bay with shade, fans, and furnaces.

▼ NATURAL WONDERS

▲ Thick cushions for leisurely lounging accent the minimal teak profile of the Poolside Armless Loveseat designed by John Hutton for **Sutherland**. This sophisticated seat is available to designers through fine showrooms nationwide.

▲ The Eighteenth-Century English Romantic Bench from **Laura Spector Rustic Design** is composed of graceful lines that follow nature's whimsy yet suggest the complexity of wrought ironwork. Crafted individually from twisted Oriental Bittersweet—a decorative woodland vine now considered an invasive weed—no two benches are exactly alike.

▲ The wide water basin of the Baluster Birdbath from **Haddonstone** will attract songbirds to your garden. Its smooth concrete curves are a work of art.

◀ Hand-carved detail embellishes the ample teak frames of the Armada Easy Chair from **Brown Jordan.** Its stately lines draw from exotic West Indies Caribbean style.

◀ Floorizon plank decking from **TimberTech** provides a low-maintenance, splinter-free surface. Made from pure plastic resins and wood fiber, this decking's long grain resembles real wood. Its tongue-and-groove engineering fits together without nails.

▶ This simple but pleasing chair and side table from **Plow and Hearth** are made from Eucalyptus—an ecofriendly hardwood with a straight grain and high oil content. Left outside year-round, its honey color will mellow to a soft gray.

◀ The tall Torrento from **Fanimation** is designed to circulate air in open spaces, making it a perfect addition to a courtyard or garden room. Weatherproof blades are woven to resemble bamboo.

◀ The rich, hand-rubbed surface of **Tropitone's** Java Table evokes a subtle tropical motif and appears to be woven from genuine, textured wicker. In reality, tabletops are molded from a single piece of high-density urethane, making them impervious to outdoor conditions.

▲ Blending robust styling with the practicality of teak, the Angulo Easy Chair from **Warisan** has large, organically shaped panels and a sleek, angular frame of highly grained plantation-grown teak.

OUTDOOR OPULENCE

▶ Cool your covered patio or porch with the Outdoor Elements collection of ceiling fans from **Hunter Fan Co.** This fan's wide, palm-shaped blades evoke refreshing tropical breezes.

▲ The Hana Road textile collection from **Perennials Outdoor Fabrics** tells a story about Hawaiian life and culture. Inspired by tropical waves, seaweed, and shells, as well as the shapes and textures of Hawaii's traditional barkcloth and kapa cloth, these contemporary patterns create an easy elegance. Fabrics are available to designers and architects through showrooms worldwide.

▲ Laid-back tropical sophistication provides the impetus for the Caribe Rocker from **Lloyd/Flanders.** Scaled for luxurious lounging, its wide, sloping wicker arms mimic the shape of overstuffed living room furniture.

▶ **Tropitone's** Lakeside Collection is designed on a generous scale to create cozy outdoor settings. The Lakeside Action Lounger has thick cushions that suggest the formality of an indoor space. Bold upholstery complements the strong geometric architecture of its aluminum frame.

◀ The opulent Wonosobo Daybed from **Warisan** is constructed from environmentally responsible recycled teak. The curved shape of its ample frame creates a gentle elegance and a wonderful place to relax.

▲ The woven Chatsworth Collection from **Brown Jordan** reinterprets traditional English garden style with an abundance of slow, elegant curves. This love seat's graciously flared arms lend to its charm, while tailored cushions provide comfort.

▲ Ask your architect or interior designer about See Sea sheer fabrics from **Perennials Outdoor Fabrics.** This light, sheer fabric in 100 percent solution-dyed acrylic has the rich look and feel of indoor fabrics but is designed to withstand outdoor elements.

▲ Vivid fabrics from **Maine Cottage** come in 148 colors and can be used to create custom pillows and cushions. Stripe Tease will stand out with bold, sophisticated strips, while Orchard presents a cocktail of fruity colors.

▼ HEAT AND SHADE

The sprightly Bella Umbrella from **Basta Sole** features a playful design with slightly flared edges, adding to its distinctive silhouette. The umbrella is available with an auto-tilt feature that allows you to control the amount of shade its canopy delivers.

◀ The fanciful Lilypond umbrella from **Santa Barbara Designs** takes its inspiration from water lilies and features cloth petals that dance in the breeze. Shown here on the stainless steel and aluminum Paseo frame, the Lilypond makes a strong design statement, especially in garden settings.

▼ Taking the chill off a cool autumn evening, patio heaters make outdoor living possible all year long. Stainless steel heaters from **Napoleon** are available in table and floor heights and feature weighted cast-iron bases for wind resistance.

▼ Used traditionally in Mexico for outdoor baking, the clay chiminea has become a popular decorative accessory that adds an earthy feel to outdoor rooms. The Kokopelli Tibor Chiminea from **Well Traveled Living** has a rustic patina and Southwestern-style engravings.

▼ The wide, retractable Isla Umbrella from **Shadescapes USA** is designed by a New Zealand sailor and features a nautical design. Its marine-grade, 100 percent solution-dyed acrylic canopy is fade-, rot-, and mold-resistant. Best of all, the Isla keeps you shaded all day long, rotating 360 degrees with a simple turn.

Tastes

Your outdoor experience is not complete without the taste of a flame-cooked feast. For savory results, equip your outdoor kitchen with appliances that suit your needs, such as a mobile grill or a complete cooking station. Today's broad range of outdoor dining sets and serving accessories will help you enjoy your spread in style.

▼ COOKING

▼ The Prestige V grill from **Napoleon** shimmers in hand-polished stainless steel. Highlights include its generous 850-square-inch (5,484 sq. cm) cooking surface and sliding storage drawers, including a top-loading drawer for dishes, buns, or towels.

▶ With a 115-volt rotisserie and an infrared rear burner, this stainless steel outdoor grill from **Wolf** is made for precision cooking. The 36-inch (91.4 cm) grill comes in freestanding and built-in models.

▲ The Gourmet-Q barbecue from **Bull Outdoor Products** is a ready-made outdoor kitchen fitted with a sink and refrigerator as well as storage drawers and plenty of counter space.

▶ The Electric Smoker Oven from **Viking** mixes heat, water vapor, and smoke for sumptuous slow cooking. Available in a built-in cabinet with a beverage center, it can stand alone as the centerpiece for a sleek outdoor kitchen.

▲ This stainless steel BBQ Collection from Eva Solo, available through **The Magazine,** has a sleek yet practical design. A set of collapsible legs supports its round steel lid, ingeniously creating a small serving table.

▲ **Charleston Gardens'** romantic cast aluminum Ashley High bistro set features scrolled chairs and a woven metal table top finished in rich natural tones. Sunbrella cushions, shown here in a neutral Sesame Linen, add a soft touch.

▲ The Zuff Collection, designed by Arik Levy for Italian manufacturer **Serralunga,** introduces colorful modern design to outdoor dining. The round, lacquered table and bar stool are available at **The Magazine.**

▲ This simple table from **Reichenberg-Weiss** is made from corrugated steel and natural French stone. Surrounded by wooden benches, it exudes a casual charm.

◄ The rattan Daisy Dining Chair from **Maine Cottage** has a light, playful form that will add whimsy to your dining table in a sunroom or covered porch.

▲ Its angular aluminium frames and sleek, minimal design distinguish the Sushi Collection from **Kristalia.** Sushi outdoor furniture adds a twist to the collection with slatted, picnic-style tops made from wide panels of high-pressure layered laminate, designed to resist ultraviolet rays.

▲ With a classic, luxurious style that bridges the gap between indoors and out, the Eden Bay dining collection from **Country Casual** is hand woven from all-weather wicker.

▶ Enjoy an al fresco snack while sitting around **Lloyd/Flanders'** Grand Traverse coffee table. A textured slate and travertine top gives the table a substantial presence, while its arched wicker base balances the mass with a lighter appearance.

▶ Graceful arches form the delicate wrought iron frames of this metal bistro table and chairs from **Haddonstone.** Their stylish figures, composed of straight, high backs and lean, lanky legs, are at home in a formal conservatory or garden.

▶ Natural, richly colored Ipe planks are framed by stainless steel for a sleek effect in **Modern Outdoor's** Etra Collection.

▼ SERVING

▲ The Alps Salad Bowl from **Cost Plus World Market** is made from hand-finished Asian hardwood, allowing you to serve your fresh creations with natural style.

▲ These gold- and copper-plated Herb Napkin Rings, designed by artist and jewelry maker Michael Michaud for **Charleston Gardens,** will add elegance to your table. Sets of four include parsley, sage, rosemary, and basil.

▶ A rustic texture defines the Bac Bac Reed Placemats from **Cost Plus World Market,** which are made from Indonesian reeds strung together with dried rope to add eclectic style to your outdoor room.

▲ The Umbrella Pole Candelabra from **Plow and Hearth** dresses up the umbrella pole to create an elegant centerpiece for your outdoor dining table.

▲ The two-tiered Copper Oval Beverage Stand from **Well Traveled Living** does double duty. A removable serving tray fits into the stand's metal frame at the top level, while a large copper bucket with a hammered finish keeps drinks cool below.

▲ The artlessly beautiful Teak Serving Set from **Country Casual** includes a pair of trivets, organically shaped serving utensils, and a broad tray that serves as a showcase for the wood's rich grain.

► The voluptuous silhouette of the Grace Pitcher from **Cost Plus World Market** makes it a clear choice for serving cold drinks.

▲ A tennis ball inspires the playful shape of the Wimbledon Tea Trolley from **Lloyd/Flanders.** Its blend of classical charm and retro style add flair to outdoor dining.

◄ Carry all of your outdoor dining necessities from the kitchen cabinet to the picnic table in one easy trip with the Wicker Picnic Organizer from **Plow and Hearth.**

▲ The striking Catalina Console, designed by Berman Rosetti for **Sutherland,** makes an excellent place to set up a buffet or bar when entertaining outdoors. Its teak frame features hand-hewn chipped detail, and the lattice detail on the lower shelf enhances its sleek, contemporary lines. The console is available to designers through fine showrooms around the world.

Directory of Design Professionals

BOORA Architects
720 SW Washington St.
Suite 800
Portland, OR 97205
Phone: 503.226.1575
Fax: 503.241.7429
www.boora.com
(12)

Tichenor & Thorp Architects
8730 Wilshire Blvd.
Beverly Hills, CA 90211
Phone: 310.358.8444
(15)

Steven Ehrlich
10865 Washington Blvd.
Culver City, CA 90232
Phone: 310.838.9700
Fax: 310.838.9737
www.s-ehrlich.com
(14, 15, 50)

Shubin + Donaldson Architects
3834 Willat Ave.
Culver City, CA 90232
Phone: 310.204.0688
Fax: 310.559.0219

1 N. Calle Cesar Chavez, Suite 200
Santa Barbara, CA 93101
Phone: 805.966.2802
Fax: 805.966.3802
www.shubinanddonaldson.com
(17, 19, 54, 55)

Eric Rosen Architects
11525 Washington Blvd.
Los Angeles, CA 90066
Phone: 310.313.3052
Fax: 310.313.3062
www.ericrosen.com
(19)

Stephen Woodhams
378 Brixton Road
London
United Kingdom
Phone: 44 (0) 020.7346.5656
www.woodhams.co.uk/
(21)

Town and Country Conservatories
1475 West Foster Ave.
Chicago, IL 60640
Phone: 773.506.8000
Fax: 773.506.8815
www.townandcountryus.com
(21, 22, 117)

Claudio Bernardes
(29)

Kanner Architects
1558 10th St.
Santa Monica, CA 90401
Phone: 310.451.5400
Fax: 310.451.5440
www.kannerarch.com
(28)

Moore Ruble Yudell Architects & Planners
933 Pico Blvd.
Santa Monica, CA 90405
Phone: 310.450.1400
Fax: 310.450.1403
www.mryarchitects.com
(25)

ORR Design Office
2319 K St. # 200
Sacramento, CA 95816
Phone: 800.647.4781
www.orrdesign.com
(43, 44, 45, 60, 61, 96, 97)

Conchita Kien
(66, 67)

Aleks Istanbullu Architects
1659 11th St.
Santa Monica, CA 90404
Phone: 310.450.8642
Fax: 310.399.1888
www.ai-architects.com
(41)

Harte, Brownlee & Associates Interior Design
1691 Westcliff Dr.
Newport Beach, CA 92660
Phone: 949.548.9530
(48)

Neumann Mendro Andrulaitis Architects, LLP
Andy Neumann
888 Linden Ave.
Carpinteria, CA 93013
Phone: 805.684.8885
Fax: 805.684.8700
www.nmaarchitects.com
(56, 57)

Kitchell Custom Homes
1700 E. Highland Ave., Suite 125
Phoenix, AZ 85016
Phone: 602.798.5700
www.kitchell.com
(59)

Architecture Plus
Mark Fredstrom
9002 North Central Ave.
Phoenix, AZ 85020
Phone: 602.264.7500
Fax: 602.277.2992
www.architectureplusltd.com
(59)

LKD Concepts
Lilia Konrad
New House Road 3
6318 Walchwil
Switzerland
Phone: 41 (0) 1758.22.49
(73)

Carlo Rampazzi
www.crandsv.com
(75)

Lighting Design International
Zero Ellaline Road
London W6 9NZ
United Kingdom
Phone: 44 (0) 20.7381.8999
Fax: 44 (0) 20.7385.0042
www.lightingdesigninternational.com
(77)

William Hefner Architecture & Interiors
Los Angeles, CA
Phone: 323.931.1365
www.williamhefner.com
(64, 122)

Wilson and Associates
8383 Wilshire Blvd.
Suite 611
Beverly Hills, CA 90211
Phone: 323.651.3234
Fax: 323.852.4758
www.wilsonassoc.com
(78, 79)

Thomas Beeton
723½ N. La Cienega Blvd.
Los Angeles, CA 90069
Phone: 310.657.5600
(83)

Randall Whitehead Lighting, Inc.
1246 18th St.
San Francisco, CA 94107
Phone: 415.626.1277
Fax: 415.255.8656
www.randallwhitehead.com
(83)

Katherine Spitz Associates Inc.
4212½ Glencoe Ave.
Marina Del Rey, CA 90292
Phone: 310.574.4460
Fax: 310.574.4462
www.katherinespitzassociates.com
(85, 89, 116, 129)

Corsini Architects
2906 Rowena Ave.
Los Angeles, CA 90039
Phone: 323.662.0752
Fax: 323.662.0754
www.corsiniarchitects.com
(86)

Courseworks
Thiskney House
2 St. James Terrace
Nottingham NG1 6FW
United Kingdom
Phone: 44 (0) 011.59.176664
(88)

Andrew and Karla Newell
(91)

Powerplant Garden Design
Scott Daigre
12693 High Winds Rd.
Ojai, CA 93023
Phone: 323.363.0844
Email: sdaigre@aol.com
(93)

Rios Clementi Hale Studios
6824 Melrose Ave.
Los Angeles, CA 90038
Phone: 323.634.9220
Fax: 323.634.9221
www.rchstudios.com
(95, 106, 107)

Marmol Radziner + Associates
12210 Nebraska Ave.
Los Angeles, CA 90025
Phone: 310.826.6222
Fax: 310.828.6226
www.marmol-radziner.com
(99, 105)

Keela Meadows
(100)

Chill Garden Design
Paul Herrington
Clay Cottage
Sturmer Road
Kedington
Suffolk CB9 7NS
United Kingdom
Phone: 44 (0) 014.40.704151
www.chillgardendesign.co.uk
(101)

Ilga Jansons and Mike Dryfoos
www.ridgegarden.org
(108, 109, 112)

McIntosh Poris Associates
36801 Woodward Ave., Suite 200
Birmingham, MI 48009
Phone: 248.258.9346
Fax: 248.258.0967
www.mcintoshporis.com
(110, 111)

Jim Reynolds
Butterfield
Ireland
Phone: 353.46.943.6017
Fax: 353.46.31702
(114)

Ursula Haldimann
and Björn Conerdings
Rahla Lakdima
Derb Mesfioui no 9,
Marrakech
Morocco
(120)

Fung + Blatt Architects
104 N. Ave. 56, Suite 3A
Los Angeles, CA 90042
Phone: 323.255.8368
Fax: 323.255.3646
www.fungandblatt.com
(126)

Michael Berman
7215 West Beverly Blvd.
Los Angeles, CA 90036
Phone: 323.933.0220
Fax: 323.933.4492
www.michaelbermanlimited.com
(128)

coLAB Studio
1614 E. Cedar St.
Tempe, AZ 85281
Phone: 480.236.0541
www.colabstudio.com
(132, 133)

MetroShed North America
David Ballinger
2721 Forsyth Road
Winter Park, FL 32792
Phone: 818.357.4000
Fax: 407.540.9687
www.metroshed.com
(134, 135)

The Garden Escape Limited
Up Beyond
Wye View Lane
Symonds Yat West
Herefordshire
HR9 6BN
United Kingdom
Phone: 44 (0) 0870.242.7024
www.thegardenescape.co.uk
enquiries@thegardenescape.co.uk
(135)

Product Sources

Ann Sacks
8120 NE 33rd Drive
Portland, OR 97211
Phone: 800.278.TILE
www.annsacks.com

Brown Jordan
9860 Gidley St.
El Monte, CA 91731
Phone: 800.743.4252
www.brownjordan.com
contact@brownjordan.com

Bull Outdoor Products
541 E Main St.
Ontario, CA 91761
Phone: 800.521.2855
www.bullbbq.com
sales@bullbbq.com

Charleston Gardens
650 King St.
Charleston, SC 29403
Phone: 800.469.0118
www.charlestongardens.com

Cost Plus World Market
Phone: 877.967.5362
www.worldmarket.com

Country Casual
7601 Rickenbacker Drive
Gaithersburg, MD 20879
Phone: 800.289.8325
Fax: 301.926.9198
www.countrycasual.com
customerservice@countrycasual.com

Fanimation
10983 Bennett Parkway
Zionsville, IN 46077
Phone: 888.567.2055
Fax: 866.482.5215
www.fanimation.com

Haddonstone (USA) Ltd.
201 Heller Place
Bellmawr, NJ 08031
Phone: 856.931.7011
Fax: 856.931.0040
www.haddonstone.com
info@haddonstone.com

Hunter Fan Co.
Phone: 800.4HUNTER
www.hunterfan.com

J Schatz
5 South Chenango St.
Greene, NY 13778
Phone: 866.344.5267
Fax: 607.656.5642
www.jshcatz.com
info@JSchatz.com

JANUS et Cie
www.janusetcie.com

KRISTALIA srl
via Calderano 5
33070 Brugnera
Italy
Phone: 39 (0) 434.23678
Fax: 39 (0) 434.624901
www.kristalia.it
info@kristalia.it

Laura Spector Rustic Design
786 Westport Turnpike
Fairfield, CT 06430
Phone: 203.254.3952
www.lauraspectorrusticdesign.com
lsrustic@aol.com

Lloyd/Flanders
3010 10th St.
PO Box 550
Menominee, MI 49858
Phone: 906.863.4494
www.lloydflanders.com

Maine Cottage
PO Box 935
Yarmouth, ME 04096
Phone: 207.846.1430
Fax: 207.846.0602
www.mainecottage.com
customerservice@mainecottage.com

Modern Outdoor
15952 Strathern St.
Van Nuys, CA 91406
Phone: 818.785.0168
Fax: 818.785.0168
www.modernoutdoors.com

Napoleon Fireplaces & Grills
24 Napoleon Road
Barrie, Ontario
L4M 4Y8
Canada
Phone: 800.461.5581
Fax: 800.667.6063
www.napoleongrills.com
info@napoleonproducts.com

Nick Williams and Associates
18751 Ventura Blvd., Suite 200
Tarzana, CA 91356
Phone: 818.996.4010
www.nickwilliamsdesigns.com

Northern Steel International
Northern Steel Business Center
Route 1
Lewes, DE 19958
Phone: 800.916.2044
Fax: 302.644.3444
www.nsteel.com
www.ecocottages.com

Open Air Designs
600 Center Ave.
Bensalem, PA 19020
www.openairdesigns.com
sales@openairdesigns.com

Serralunga
Via Serralunga 9
13900 Biella
Italy
Phone: 39 (0) 15.2435711
Fax: 39 (0) 15.31081
www.serralunga.com
info@serralunga.com

Perennials Outdoor Fabrics
3225 E. Carpenter Freeway
Irving, TX 75062
Phone: 888.322.4773
Fax: 214.420.1600
www.perennialsfabrics.com

Plow and Hearth
Phone: 800.494.7544
www.plowhearth.com

Reichenberg-Weiss
Pascalstrasse 17
Neukirchen-Vluyn
Germany
Phone: 49 (0) 284598.08.00
Fax: 49 (0) 284598.08.10
www.reichenberg-weiss.de
info@reichenberg-weiss.de

Santa Barbara Designs
PO Box 6884
Santa Barbara, CA 93160
Phone: 800.919.9464
Fax: 805.683.9468
www.sbumbrella.com
info@sbumbrella.com

ShadeScapes USA
PO Box 190
39300 Back River Rd.
Paonia, CO 81428
Phone: 866.997.4233
Fax: 970.527.7082
www.shadescapesusa.com
info@shadescapesusa.com

Sutherland
168 Regal Row
Dallas, TX 75247
Phone: 800.717.8325
www.sutherlandteak.com

The Magazine
1823 Eastshore Highway
Berkeley, CA 94710
Phone: 510.549.2282
www.themagazine.info
themag@pacbell.net

The Nantucket Post Cap Company
44 Hull St.
Randolph, VT 05060
Phone: 888.758.POST
www.nantucketpostcap.com
info@NantucketPostCap.com

TimberTech
894 Prairie Ave.
Wilmington, OH 45177
Phone: 800.307.7780
www.timbertech.com

Tropitone Furniture Co., Inc.
5 Marconi
Irvine, CA 92618
Phone: 949.595.2000
www.tropitone.com

Viking
Phone: 888.VIKING1
www.vikingrange.com

Warisan
7470 Beverly Blvd.
Los Angeles, CA 90036
Phone: 877.WARISAN
Fax: 323-938-3959
www.warisan.com
lasales@warisan.com

Wolf
Phone: 800.332.9513
www.subzero.com/wolf

Well Traveled Living
PO Box 4
716 South 8th St.
Amelia Island, FL 32034
Phone: 904.261.5400
Fax: 904.261.6769
www.wtliving.com
sales@welltraveled.net

YLighting
Phone: 888.888.4449
www.ylighting.com

...nting, Inc.,

...esign Office, Inc.,
...01

Laurie Black,
12

Tom Bonner
Shubin + Donaldson Architects,
54; 55

Don Button
ORR Design Office, Inc.,
43 (bottom); 44 (top); 45; 96; 97

Weldon Brewster
Aleks Istanbullu Architects,
40

Ciro Coelho,
17; 19 (bottom)

Grey Crawford,
14; 15 (top)

Scott Daigre
Powerplant Garden Design,
93

Guillaume DeLaubier,
10; 32; 35; 57 (bottom); 70; 82; 115; 119 (top); 125; 130

Carlos Domenech,
9; 38; 98; 127

John Ellis,
99; 105

John Ellis
Rios Clementi Hale Studios,
95; 106 (bottom); 107

David Glomb,
86; 87

Reto Guntli,
zapaimages
www.zapaimages.com,
23 (bottom); 27 (bottom); 36; 39; 66; 67; 69; 73; 74; 75 (bottom); 80; 81; 84; 106 (top); 120; 121; 129 (top)

Courtesy of William Hefner Architecture & Interiors,
64; 122

Aleks Istanbullu
Aleks Istanbullu Architects,
41

Nicholas Kane,
Alamy Images
www.alamy.com,
22 (bottom)

Balthazar Korab
McIntosh Poris Associates,
110; 111

Erich Ansel Koyama,
19 (top)

Steve LaCap
Katherine Spitz Associates, Inc.,
85 (bottom); 89; 104; 116; 129 (bottom)

John Edward Linden,
28

Sylvia Martin,
23 (top); 34 (top); 43 (top); 44 (bottom); 62; 63 (bottom); 94

Courtesy of MetroShed,
134; 135 (bottom)

Shelley Metcalf,
5; 13; 26; 34 (bottom); 46; 47; 58; 59 (top); 85 (top); 92; 103; 119 (bottom)

Yvonne Neumann
Neumann Mendro Andrulaitis Architects, LLP,
56; 57 (top)

Clive Nichols
www.clivenichols.com,
11 (bottom); 21 (bottom); 42; 52; 75 (top); 77; 88; 91; 100; 101; 108; 109; 112; 113; 114; 124

Jurgen Nogai
Steven Ehrlich Architects,
50

Eric Roth,
72

Scott Sandler
Kitchell Contractors,
59 (bottom)

Agi Simoes,
zapaimages
www.zapaimages.com,
29; 51

Tim Street-Porter,
6; 15 (bottom); 18; 20; 48; 49; 63 (top); 71; 76; 78; 79; 83 (top); 90; 102; 123; 126; 128

Courtesy of The Garden Escape Limited,
134 (top)

Bill Timmerman
coLAB Studio,
132; 133

Courtesy of Town & Country Conservatories,
21 (top); 22 (top); 117

Courtesy of Warisan
www.warisan.com,
27; 37

Dennis Welch
Courtesy of Maine Cottage Furniture,
11 (top)

Conrad White,
zapaimages
www.zapaimages.com,
24

Deborah Whitlaw Llewellyn,
16; 31; 33; 118

Bill Zeldis
Neumann Mendro Andrulaitis Architects, LLP,
65

Scot Zimmerman,
30; 53; 68; 131; 136

Kim Zwarts
Moore Ruble Yudell Architects & Planners,
25

Acknowledgments

To everyone who made *Outdoor Rooms II* an exciting and educational experience, th. you. The architects, interior designers, landscape architects, furniture manufacturers, an. photographers whose work is featured in its pages deserve recognition for their creativity, which truly makes the world a more beautiful place to live. My talented Quarry editors, Candice Janco and Betsy Gammons, who experienced the triumphs and travails of the project alongside me, have been invaluable resources. This book is evidence of their wise advice and great skill in gathering spectacular photos. Special thanks are due also to Julie D. Taylor for introducing me to the thrilling worlds of design and publishing, and providing an inspirational foreword that I'm honored to have as a part of my first book. My closest friends and family—Mike, Sherry, Jill, David Dickhoff, and Oscar Ramallo—receive my deepest love and gratitude for their encouragement as I undertook this project and their patience during the intense weeks of writing. Thank you, Grandma Pat, for the lounge chair that steered me down the path to outdoor decorating; and thank you, Grandma Joyce, for sharing your sense of style. Finally, thank you, reader, for buying my book.

Author

Anne Dickhoff grew up in northern California, where her first outdoor room was a tent in the Sierra Nevada Mountains. She became passionate about design while working as a marketing writer for architects, furniture manufacturers, and builders. Her articles on architecture and product design have been featured in *Desire Los Angeles* and *Desert Living* magazine. Anne currently lives in Phoenix, Arizona. *Outdoor Rooms II* is her first book.